Trees of Surprise

Marjorie Norris, Editor

BlazeVOX [books]

Buffalo, New York

The Trees of Surprise by Marjorie Norris

Published by BlazeVOX [books]

Printed in the United States of America

Book design by Geoffrey Gatza

First Edition

ISBN: 1-934289-6 ISBN 13: 978-1-934289-66-2
Library of Congress Control Number: 2007931778
Cover Art Priscilla Bowen, "Unexpected"

BlazeVOX [books]
14 Tremaine Ave
Kenmore, NY 14217

Editor@blazevox.org

publisher of weird little books

BlazeVOX [books]

blazevox.org

2 4 6 8 0 9 7 5 3 1

Table of Contents

Poems are made by fools like me,

But only God can make a tree.

From "Trees" by Joyce Kilmer (1886-1918)

Dedication

> *"And the wind said:*
> *May you be as strong as the oak,*
> *yet flexible as the Birch,*
> *may you stand tall as the Redwood,*
> *live gracefully as the Willow,*
> *and may peace and prosperity*
> *surround you all of your days."*
>
> *Tree of Life Inspirations*
> *www.treeol.com*

I'd like to thank Anne Ritenour for her original view of this book and help at its start, also Liz Walczak for her gracious response to written contributions and photographs, to Tim Maggio and Kathy Mecca as well as my children Marie Norris-Baxter and Mark Norris and Mark's wife, Michelle Norris, for being there to support the community's Karpele's Museum event on October 13, 2007, the first anniversary of the Trees of October Surprise. Much appreciation for the remarkable talent of Priscilla Bowen, whose paintings grace the cover and inside of this anthology and Linda Lavid, for her part in cover design. Gratitude to Talia Roth for her remarkable photograph on the back. Much thanks to Just Buffalo Literary Center, Arts Council in Buffalo and Erie County, Buffalo News and Artvoice, local radio and TV stations, Talking Leaves and Barnes and Noble as well as amazon.com for getting the word out. And thank you, all, contributors throughout Western New York and other climes, you know who you are, and all you mean to me. May we be strengthened in our loss of the trees and our appreciation for them, wise ancestors all.

Marjorie Norris, editor, Trees of Surprise*
Author of Two Suns, Two Moons, Aventine Press, 2005*
Resilience, Aventine Press 2007*

*All available at Talking Leaves Bookstore, Buffalo, New York or amazon.com

Introduction

I want to thank all the Western New Yorkers who have presented their wonderful writing, art and photographs to create this anthology. These words celebrate our lost trees and remember the trees that have meant so much to us in our childhoods and beyond.

It seems trees hold our strength for us, some of our internal world, as well as the outer. They are great archetypes. Trees are loved, painted, photographed, sat and made love under, climbed in, and hugged. Trees are, as humans can be, large and lofty. And babies, in their buggies, stare up and out into the wide sky through the kaleidoscopic canopies of their leaves.

Many spring days, strolling around the periphery of the golf course at Delaware Park, I have walked so enjoyably and long as to find the March trees seeming to walk toward me, rather than I toward them. Of course, this is an optical illusion, as when the Niagara River seems still and I, the watcher, seem to be moving South just looking at it. These are the wonders of our earth and water, our steadfast roots and images. We have lost so much of them, yet nature has provided more.

May it always be this way.

Marjorie Norris, Editor

Trees of Surprise will be available for sale at the first anniversary celebration and book signing Saturday, October 13, 2007 at Karpele's Museum, 453 Porter Avenue, Buffalo, New York 14201. The time is 4 pm to 6 pm. Each one of our contributors will receive a complimentary copy for their writing or photos, and others will be available for sale at a nominal price. Remember, they make great holiday gifts!

Trees of Surprise

One of the Many Fine Times

Priscilla Bowen

October 13, 2006

It was so beautiful the morning of the storm. I proudly pointed out to a visitor that the broad-armed maple on our front lawn was at the height of its color. He agreed, it was an exquisite sight. Later in the day I stood on the porch watching the rain coat the grass and leaves, and was delighted by the reds and oranges and sunny yellows glazed by a thin, clear film of ice. It was a shimmering fairy world.

Then I heard the first crack. Startling, loud. It came from the next block. And then another crack. This one seemed to come from just down the street. Soon another and another until I was afraid the neighborhood was falling apart. The splintering noise alarmed me and I hid inside.

All evening and night and into the next day, sounds like a bullwhip on bare flesh, over and over again. From the window I watched the arch of trees above the street fall in on itself. And our lovely maple, limb after limb, arms breaking off at the shoulders, its decades of nurtured symmetry interrupted by the sudden exposure of harsh, black, anorexic elbows pointing to the sky.

It was dreadful and frightening. Helpless tears wet my cheeks. From enchantment to grief in such a short time.

Madeline Davis
Williamsville, New York

red bud

she stood near our front door
where she housed the finches
and welcomed the paper boy
late afternoons when neighbors dropped by
she looked fragile and shy unlike the oaks and elms
around the yard's perimeter
but strong nonetheless—
she outlived by years
dire warnings of landscape professionals
who saw her as half-dead

her arms stretched across the front yard
when her tiny blossoms burst through their shells
each May we were startled into spring
then lulled through summer's heat
with her cooling shade
even in winter the twinkling lights
wrapped around her branches kept our spirits high

it will be hard now
to mark the seasons
without her
hard to recognize soft changes
without this friend

Margaret Cusack
Williamsville, NY

Smallest Tree, Largest Love

In the garden, shaped like a pentagon,
The two foot tree stands half-fallen,
She shows no fear,
Her bark is gray and frail
She breathes small breaths with hesitation
But shows no blossom
She stares into the sun
If she fails, she'll rest in peace
Knowing she was ours

Chelsea Blackman
Age: 11, Clarence, NY
Student of Margaret Cusack, Ledgeview Elementary School

Dance for the Trees

(for Stan)

Tree- half blooming with bursting, luxuriating pink blossoms

- half dead from the storm

Leaning my head and belly into her
"What do you feel" I ask

It was a shift for us
A chance to move into new forms
You have been through such a shift
Our dead limbs mean as much to us as your old baggage to you

Our life force moves into new paths, the living limbs
We know new vitality, new eddies of energy

She pulls me to her blooming side
So that I can feel it in my body

Anne Marie Worthy
Buffalo, New York

October Surprise

In that melancholy time of late afternoon
The snow begins
Falls through the stained glass colors
Of October leaves
Floats slowly down like quiet dreams
Builds in drifts along the branches
Piles around thick trunks
Weighs down the brilliant leaves
Deeper and deeper
Through the night the darkness fills with
Staccato cracks and crashes,
Snow thunder and wind
Finally silence returns and
In a stark morning light the trees stand crippled
With broken leafless branches and
Shattered bodies remnants
Of their once strong and beautiful selves
Wood still alive with
Years of struggle and growth

They seem surprised themselves and
Their surprise echoes our own
At the shock and grief we feel
Surprise at our sense of shared pain and loss
Surprise at our new sense of
Their importance in our lives

Sally Johnson
Gasport, New York

Haiku

Crimson, bronze, gold fire
In snow they fall like ashes
New life for tired earth

Sally Johnson
Gasport, NY

March Willows

A white cold wind
Whips around the trees
Forces even *stay-all-winter* geese
To hide huddled under the canal bridge
Against a pewter sky   willow branches
Catch and hold a few scattered glimpses of
Pale sun
Ice-tipped and brittle   brown buds
Swell under a colorless frosty glaze
Lustrous yellow stems wave
In frantic spiral patterns

Everyone else has given up
The summer garden lays lifeless
Wild raspberries and bare shrubs bend low
Under still deep snow
Small creatures in
Tiny winter homes
Sleep on and on
But the willow trees know it's March
The willow trees believe in Spring

Sally Johnson
Gasport, NY

Nests

They are webbed firmly into the crook
Of branches tested by winds and snow---
By storms blowing in fast from the lake
To crash scree against the shore.
Branches crack and sliver off
But still the abandoned nests hold--
Those dried twigs strapped together
Weaved as monuments
To families grown and gone:
Yet they still wait.

Linda Drajem
Buffalo, NY

Our City Trees

Clipped and shaved heads
Tortured by storm and by neglect
They wave black arms in snow-laden streets
With raw wounds of sawed branches.
Bony limbs left to rot
Turn inward to meditate on loss
And if blame, then that too.
Like our city they were abandoned
To send out wild leaves each spring
In streams of air exhaled from factories
Trying to keep a city alive,
The rush of tramping feet
Bleeds energy that has weaned us
From savoring those bowers
Those umbrella shoulders that shelter
And keep strong hope.
Now the cracked and crazed trees tell our story.

Linda Drajem
Buffalo, New York

Loblolly Pine

A name derived from "moist depressions"
Also "thick gruel" or "muddy mire"
Now favors bottomlands in the South
Grows dense and tall near the Gulf
But dreams of sisters up North—
Frozen pine and spruce
Burdened with snow and weak roots
Squared jaw against the blizzard
Eager to hold but wind-tossed

No *lob lollying* in this climate
No relaxing by a golf course
Or serenading a constant sun
To whistle in gentle breezes
Accompanied by a cicada orchestra
These sisters and brothers too
Stand tall away from depressions
Stand firm and only lollygag
When spring arrives to hint of southern air

Linda Drajem
Buffalo, New York

The Shadow at the Core

The apples were green,
Too tart and small to eat,
But Grandma lapped them
In her bib apron and
Made sweet, juicy strudels.
This was her humble tree,
Not the kind to entice Snow White
Or harbor serpents.

That is why the
Man in the Brown Hat
Startled us,
Showing up so brazenly
One Tuesday night
Under Grandma's apple tree.

His long shadow
Crept toward our window
As if knowing Mom was out
Bowling at Lucky Strike Lanes,
As if seeing Dad with his
Wrinkled brown bag
Leave for the graveyard shift
At Bethlehem.

Yes, while lights flickered
Black and white inside and
Our little heads whirled with
Tales from Alcoa Presents,
The Man in the Brown Hat
Broke into Grandma's tree
And stood his ground.

What a long night it was,
Left as we were in
P.J.'s, our only armor.
Nowhere to hide,
No fairy godmother to
Stop the invader...
And, in hindsight,
Nothing did stop the siege.

Though summers of apples
Continued tumbling onto
Doughy laps,
The tree itself never did grow taller,
While the silhouette of the
Man in the Brown Hat
Seemed to swell, spilling
Over picnics and
Puddles of apples,
Now turning brown,
Under Grandma's Apple Tree.

Carol Pasiecznik
Buffalo, New York

Lilac Tree

"Is that snow, love, clinging to the limbs of the tree, or
warm sleeves of light instead?" Quavering, uncertain
she spoke. Their love, intently studied under the microscope,
is cracked and its patina is worn thin.

Surprisingly, snow fell in October this year.
Trunks split from the weight and
Branches hang like impotent members
Of an arboreal army.

Daily, as the sun pushed the horizon away
Like an unwelcome guest,
Another Woman snuck quietly into their home.
Always the Gentleman, He held the door open for Her.
Legs splayed like broken limbs
They tainted history on the living room floor.

Now alone, she sits in her home.
Gazing out at the soft,
Budding potential of her cherished lilac tree.
Wavering sleeves of light diffract through
The bubbled glass and feel warm on her face.

Anonymous
Buffalo, NY

My Yggdrasil

You reach into the world
From the place I set you to earth,
A twig that shouldn't have lasted a winter,
Now scraping the bottoms of clouds,
Rooted below the world,
Deeper than I've grown,
And towering above me, ages old.

How can that be? I planted you
In my lifetime,
            Liar!

Are you my *axis mundi,*
Grown beyond expectation?
And I, who stand at your base,
Am I so much older
Than the child who planted you,
Climbed you before your time?

How long ago
Did I set dry twig to earth?
Am I ancient now?
You've outgrown my reach
In brief decades, left me on earth
While you ascended the sky.
Who'll climb you now?

Go back and be a twig again;
Grow when it suits you.
I'll be waiting to climb you
When you're ready. I won't be
Too old by then,

Yggdrasil,
World Tree,
Liar!

David Park Musella
Amherst, New York
Center for Inquiry's coordinator
Literary events, first Wednesday of month

The October Day

The October day,
The Snowmen came to town.

They took our trees
And sat on their crowns.

Breaking their limbs,
All straight down.

The snowmen's convention was short.
They stayed but three days.

The mess they left,
Kept us in the dark for a week.

Years will be needed,
To replace the trees they sat upon.

The Snowmen's early convention
Dealt with Mother Nature's pruning.

They were swift with their decisions,
Took no deliberations.

With a little thunder from above,
And a lot of snapping below, they were done.

The snowmen adjourning, said "We had
Great fun." They asked their Council
"What year will we be returning?"

Larry Bachman
Buffalo, NY

Visualize

Along the path in the park, walking,
With this child, alongside, a long, slender sapling.
Still bare of buds, still, undressed for spring,
Looks to us, from the middle distance. Walking,
We look at it. We see, the breeze does, too.
Breaths of it, brush, first, the crown, then, the branch
Beneath. Points of small, sharp shapes, in close,
Clustered groups, in either place, each one, still, till,
Then, now, pushed to move, nudges the other. Each
One, then, to please the other, flutters

Pumping my hand, now, the child cries, "Look! See. See.
Look. There in the trees, BIRDIES. Hello!" she says, "Hello!
You say, hello, too," she says. Complying, "Hello, Birdies,"
I reply. Close-up, now, what I see, at the crown, the cluster of
Dark, dried leaves, winter's leavings, these, the close-knit group.
Beneath, on the branch, scraps of paper, these, twig on twig, hooked.
All these, small, sharp points, at a distance, to us, the tips of wings,
The clutch of these, settled in the tree, our birds in a rook

About to say, what I know she sees, now, this springs to mind:
"See with the child's eyes. If you look, insist, she, merely, look,
she will never see. Never, again, will she VISUALIZE."

Joanna Dicker-Bachman
Buffalo, NY

Lights Out

On the evening of our unseasonable snowstorm
We were thrown into wilderness time
Dropped, without provisions, in the middle of cold and dark
A timelessness that created a weird sense of calm,
So we retreated to our bed, heaped high with blankets
And fat oblivious cats for comfort.
We ate tuna sandwiches by candlelight.
We tuned in to the Talk Radio station.
We heard voices fussing, complaining,
Operating at a level that reptilian brains resort to
When they are faced with the sudden inconvenience
Of no heat and no lights.
The room became our bomb shelter, keeping out
The alien saunas of hail pellets peppering the windows
And odd lightning piercing a pink sky, and in the snow-
Muffled morning, we dodged the remains of shocked,
Ruined trees, many still in full fall splendor
And we mourned, as if they were casualties of war:
Their thin, pitiful arms and massive split trunks all
Succumbed to the weight of heavy snows. Here,
Nature laid her burden down, with branches at our feet,
Laying waste the trees, the pride of our city to scream
A message to us, that we can no longer afford to ignore
Her warnings.

Joni Russ
Buffalo, NY
Peace activist, environmentalist

Going

I'll never forget peering out my second-story window
At my old friend: he was tall, round, and stretched
Out towards the threatening sky, for years he stood
Strong and weathered elements year after year, but
Today it was unseasonably cold and wet. I peered
Through my window in wonderment, what would be
The fate of my large towering friend? The weather
Made a turn for the worse and all I could hear
Was crackin' and snappin': the snow was falling
Hard and the ice was forming fast, his weighted
Branches began to plummet into the white abyss
Below. I pondered the fate of my friend, whom
Should I call and as I thought, he stood strong
And tall, sleep fell over and everything
Was eerily quiet, a white softness blanketed
The noise. I sprang out of bed and my bare feet
Dipped into the unusual crisp morning air....
Not a thing was moving, just the sound of still
Atmosphere. I looked out the window and gasped
With relief: my old friend was still standing
But not without despair. As I saw him anew,
I assured myself he would continue to grow,
Because he must be two hundred years old
And surely he had felt this many times before.
I smiled, I had to go.

Marty Lougen
Buffalo, NY

The Crown

Crown: top of your head (I had a cowlick there once)
Crown: a symbol of royalty
Crown: on a tooth
Crown: the top of trees

You can break the crown of your head and recover (hopefully)
You can die and pass the crown of royalty on
You can save the tooth with a crown (your choice, gold or silver)
But once the crown on the tree dies so does the tree.

Michael Villar
Kenmore, NY

Into the Perfect Air of October

The wish of burning brings me here.
I forego tunnels and greetings
From past loves and the embrace
Of the one who may only love me.
I choose to lie in the snow though
Of forest floor where carbon chains cleave
And rains dissolve my elements. I arise
Through blackened wicks of trunks
Into the green body of spring. As the light
Of summer lapses, weather cools, and bird
Flocks take on direction, my wish follows:
I burn in the golden flames of trees—
In candle beyond candle—as my last breath
Passes into the perfect air of October

James Sedwick
South Wales, New York

Autumnal Virgin Storm

night falls and
an early winter wind
filled with shards of white
speaks to me
of a bitter earthly ache

in my bed
do not watch me as I hide
beneath blankets of autumn
listening to the blows in restless sleep

he arrived burnished and angry
with his whip vicious
exuding his relentless pressure
on heavy bended limbs

cries calling out in the darkness
for moonbeams to wrap them in comfort
and I lay here
wishing for someone to stop the torture of Mary

throw no more stones
for she is clean

send a caregiver to bind her wounds
give her another chance
to become a new world of light and dawn
and fill her tender ears with hope

she wanders on toward Nazareth
trudging forward in mourning
for the angels ripped from us
without notice

Denise Amodeo Miller
Kenmore, NY

Sunshine

Raindrops falling trickling down
Washing me and nourishing me round
Rejoice should I or sadden?
That what brings me life cannot!

So barren so brown I stand
Staring at the dark blue gray sky
Expecting answers to my rhetorical why!
"Why does that which brings me life cannot?"

Upset and frightened, I prepare
For the cold coming from the north
Waiting for this time to pass!
Resolute shall I stand or fall
In the dream of that splendid sunshine?

Amrutansh Salunkhe
Williamsville, NY

Crazy in October

The storm
With the sound of
Tree limbs and branches
Cracking all around
Like gunfire

The generators like base camp

The devastation of the trees
Like a war zone

Another heart
Momentarily shattered

Cameo
Buffalo, NY

They are All Willows

Weeping
Heaviness

Buck shot thunder
Shatters bone

Jagged limbs
Spear the sky

Strange and piercingly
Quiet.

Lisa Forrest
Buffalo, NY

A Winter Afternoon, and Everyone Sighing

Today, the trees
tangled up torn
stand gilded silver

shimmering graceful
between the sun
and eyes blind

a winter
afternoon
and everyone

sighing
for something
different from yesterday

once you said
before
doesn't exist anymore

and I thought
I loved
everything.

Lisa Forrest
Buffalo, NY

For Leslie

Our big, beautiful, backyard tree
Came down during the surprise 2006
October snowstorm, the same day
As our seventh wedding anniversary,
As a matter of fact. Friday the 13th
To be exact.

Our big, beautiful, backyard tree,
Providing shade for our garden.
Remember when it once shaded
Your huge backyard pool?
Our insurance company lost our
Claim, and we got no help from
Them until last month.

So our big, beautiful, backyard tree
Still lies upon the ground where it
Fell, now our yard has no shade. It
Just has huge tree limbs lying over
Two-thirds of our lawn and garden.
We dream of planting sunflowers
In the garden, welcoming the sun
Like soldiers standing tall.

Part of our big, beautiful, backyard tree
Still stands. We had high hopes of it
Blooming in spring, but alas,
It is dead. Towering over two large
Garages, this dead tree serves as a
Reminder of that nasty (but beautiful)
October storm, when it snowed and snowed
Until our big, beautiful, backyard tree
Could not bear any more weight
And thundered to the ground,
Splitting into pieces.

We shall miss it greatly when they
Finally put it to rest, grinding it
Down to pulp.

Joanna Cole, born on Valentine's Day, 1954, in Cleveland, Ohio, now resides in Buffalo, NY with her partner Leslie. She is sustained by goddess worship, art, poetry, gardening, bird watching, and her pet dog, Pinky.

Tumbling

There is more to fear
In a cradled crescent night
Than the thought of promises
Being broken by a lover
Aching to kiss another.

Dreams, like nightmares,
Get caught in the leaves of trees
Hidden behind the daylight,
Needing to be touched and
Shaped by gentle hands
Until frost sets them free.

Nightmares, as these dreams,
Are hiding behind the daylight
Fading with dawn's crescent moon,
Tumbling to the ground in Fall
Where you lay naked under the trees.
The leaves caress your skin,
Not sure if this peacefulness
Will be broken by a nightmare's promise
Or a lover's moonlight dream.

A warm October sun heats up your mushroom skin.
A soft breeze from the South lifts and separates
The leaves from where they want to stay.

Down. Down. Down,
The last leaf of Fall.
Nightmare tumbling or
Dream tumbling,
Hiding behind nature's kiss.

Down. Down. Down,
The last leaf of Fall
Upon your wanting belly.
Its hard curved stem alive
In our scented garden.
Perfumed by love.
Moistened by lust.

Which fear will you leave behind
As it enters your womb and
Wraps itself around your heart.

Wayne Ray
London, Ontario, Canada

Locust

When he found her, barely breathing,
Bound to the trunk of the Black Locust,
He pulled her spine pricked body down
To rest on the green green grass, red
Blood seeping slowly from her white skin.

On her back, on the ground, breathing.
He slowly lay her down, breathing,
And wondered how and when and why.

The blue sky will tell no secrets,
The wind listens but has blown by.
Rocks and trees absorb words but he
Could not see past bloodstained skin, and wept.

This hard pain, locust needle pricking,
Willows weeping, pines pining, spruce
Gum forming amber while Dawn Redwood
Gave up her branches to heal the wounds.

He placed her on the back, on the grass
And laid the redwood branches to cover
Her skin and pain and watched in quiet awe
As they absorbed the red blood and stains.

And though she was alive and free
Of the locusts' barbed black kiss,
She awoke under the star-filled sky,
Coils of rope still tied to her wrists.

Wayne Ray
London, Ontario, Canada
Wayne was instrumental in establishing London Arts Council, and has won many awards for his writing throughout Canada. His latest book of short stories and poetry was published in 2006 by Harmonia Press.

Bliss

Watched them fall today

October's fierce breath
Blown across the Eastern shore
Mingled with waters, warm
Creating tears of ice
As that of a monument marking graves
An angel's gaze, frozen in marble

Their limbs crack and bleed
Seeping years of kids climbing
Birds and squirrels no more to berth
Within a canopy of peace

-they had no choice but to flee—

and the workers slave
covered in sap, debris
tying rope around neck
pulling root from dirt from Earth

circles of years
staring to snow cloud skies
still breathing
still alive

O, Mother! Hold me close.

Your children weep within my chest
Hidden deep within my throat

They scream
Knowing full well
They shall rebirth
More wood for their fires

I am witness to a crucifixion

Yet it makes me ponder
These rugged soldiers
Both men and maple

--a holocaust of insurmountable proportion—

and watch with despair
crews assemble arms legs limbs hair and

blud

    blud

        blud

sap stuck
to gloves

--modern day Romans—

the only difference:
the wrinkled brows and dress
obvious distress
on each face
as they feed their Mother's breast

to the chipper.

Susan Marie
Buffalo, NY

Forest Lawn Fall Morning

How lucky I am to have this incredibly beautiful old cemetery in my neighborhood! This is not just a place for the dead, it is a garden, a park, an arboretum, it is full of art and beauty and magic. And I can go here every morning to take walks and let myself be completely enchanted over and over again. It doesn't matter what time of the year I go there, it is always mystical and full of beauty. Right now it is clothed in all its fall splendor. I went this morning while great gusts of wind were blowing, yet the sun was shining and the skies were blue. Leaves were dancing in a frenzy through the air, but many, many were still on the trees, and the ground was covered with them. Where there was green grass last week there is now a thick carpet of golden leaves and the sun is shining through branches still covered in gold high up. And I feel like Alibaba walking through the treasure cave or an elf from Rivendale. But then I come to the next section, and here are trees that seem to be on fire in their red and orange hues. And then there are the unfortunate ones that just turn from green to brown. But even in that brown there are sparkle tones of shimmering copper light once I look a little closer. Nature puts much care and beauty into dying here, and I feel very blessed to be allowed to witness it in such a splendid place where I discover something new almost every day. Even if it is just a leaf on fire that I can't help but must pick it up to take it home, I put it in my heavy thousand page book on gardening. That way I have it in the winter when everything is void of color, a little splash of fire when I open the book to make plans for my garden in the spring.

Sabine Van Wyck Haney
Buffalo, NY

Remains of winter

on a late spring morning
when the day stays so long
it almost greets the next
I look into the sky quickly
to see the remains of winter
for they disappear in a breath
the time of periwinkle light
surrounding Chantilly lace trees
whose ebony knots and threads
whisper at dawn
like prayers at vespers
whose branches jangle
like the chains of crystal rosaries of winter nuns
leaving hard white beds and stony gray walls
in the bruise of twilight

Barbara Faust, teacher
Buffalo, NY
Bennett Park Montessori School

"Fall"ing Trees

This story is about when a snow storm hit Buffalo and surprised everybody! I went for a walk with my mom and her friend. While we were walking we found many different kinds of sticks, twigs, and woods. Our pockets were full!!

Oh! I forgot to tell you about the storm.

My mom had a meeting at our house and when they walked out the door we saw a fallen tree on our lawn. There were buckets and buckets of snow in my neighborhood. The next morning trees were everywhere! They were on top of cars, covering lawns, and blocking the middle of streets and driveways.

Early in the morning me and my mom and my next door neighbors all pushed wood, and trimmed wood, and shoveled the snow. I brushed off our car. The garage was closed (where the shovels were) so I used a sweep broom. Both sides of the broom were helpful to me. The best trick to get the snow off was to use the handle and shove it into the snow on the car. Then I pushed the handle to the side and lifted it up and pushed. Then I kept going until the car was done.

We didn't have any electricity. That means we didn't have lights, television, hot water, heat, telephone, or anything that you need to plug into an outlet.

Me and my mom packed clothes, sleeping bags, and food and brought it to our friend's apartment. Her refrigerator was packed with food—food—food! We slept there for four nights (except one night I had a sleepover at Hannah Rose Leiber's house). We had fun together. Hannah had electricity.

We went for a walk after dinner one night and collected some of the sticks, twigs, and wood. My favorite things I collected were shredded up wood, the inner bark, the outer back, and the inside of the branches.

This was the storm that closed Tapestry Charter School and many more schools. What I will remember the most is that I was studying trees at the same time.

Love,

Bessie

Bessie Shiroki, age 7-1/2
Buffalo NY
Tapestry School

Trees

I love trees, paper, wood, and animals.
Trees hold animals, nests and more.
Trees, trees, trees, what more?
They can be hurt and killed,
But most of all, they are my friends!

Taylor Mossman
Our Lady of the Blessed Sacrament School, Depew, NY

Trees

Grow the food we eat

O R A N G E S

B A N A N A S

P R E T T Y - F U L L

We use trees

In our

EVERYDAY LIFE
Paper

Pencils

Justin Frost
Cheektowaga, NY
Our Lady of the Blessed Sacrament School, Depew, NY

Trees

Tumbling
Down
Crack crack crack
Splintering
Boooooom
To the ground.
Wires
Hot, cold
Draped
Across
The snowscape.
Power of Mother Nature.

Anne Ritenour
Buffalo NY

October Storm Surprise

Winter crash
Ice, snow.
Trees with leaves
Fall colors
Did not arrive.

Anne Ritenour
Buffalo, NY

No More Pears

Twenty years ago you were said to be past your prime
But we pruned and nurtured with the hope for fruit just one more time
The next spring there were buds and blossoms galore
With help from a special spray sold at the local feed store
Nay-sayers laughed and taunted "You'll never get fruit"
But I sprayed and we watched for signs of fall loot!
From buds to small fruit we watched as they grew
And the children and I planned to can, eat and share the whole slew
For many years your pears graced our table and filled the pantry shelves
You helped us to feed others and not just ourselves
No more fallout for the deer or refuge for the turkeys to roost
Or a familiar resting spot for a tired Canada goose,
Now your branches are broken, with the good old days gone
But the joy that you've given us in our memories lives on

Liz Walczak
Lancaster, NY

In Recognition and Reverence

Heartwood divine,
        Maple presence.

Treasured being,
        Loved with ease.

You hold all memory in your carbon,

Casting last year's shadow
        Far beyond this winter's reach.

Elizabeth Stone
Buffalo, NY

Bees

Bees leave
Leaves leave
Rains freeze
Trees bend
Limbs descend
To the ground

CRACKING LOUD

Echoes down
The creek bed

Susan Keleher
Lockport, NY

Waiting

Fears lie in the waiting.
It was like that with October's trees:
The weight of ice mounting steadily
A crystal Halloween disguise
Encasing the night
Mimicking my breath
Frozen in silence.....
Poised like a rabbit's ears.
That tidal interval between
What was and what will be
Is the moment we are most alive.
When the weight of death brushed
Seductively up against us...
The trees skyward yearning
Snapped! in an instant
And splintered cries fell smothered
At the soft breasts of the earth.

Susan Keleher
Lockport, NY

Poplars

Silent soldiers they stand
Exposed to all, taken for granted
Living, motionless, chilled
Catching the moon's radiance
At their tip, their shadows
Elongated.

A scene in solitude: they
Are seemingly content
To fulfill a purpose.

Linda A. King
Tonawanda, NY

Trees

Oh, if these trees would live in me,
Then I would be their Buddha soul
Silent, still
    In seasons, new and old
    In weather, fair our foul.

If these trees would live in me,
I'd speak the brittle truth of bark
Absorb the words of wind without response.
And learn love's patient presence.

If these trees would live in me,
Branch and trunk would rooted be
In sacred soil of myself
Where indwelling Spirit breathes.

If these trees would live in me
Always my guests they would be.
I'd raise my arms to welcome
Their endless branches in surrender.

Evelyn F. Brady
Buffalo, NY

A Sudden Loss
(For William Mace)

There are trees that have been with us all our lives.
They are often there before we are.
A permanent fixture in our lives.
Often something that we find comfort
And often joy in

We climb them when we are small.
We hide under them when we are grown.
They nurture us, often supplying sustenance
And guidance.

And then one day,
A great tumult
Takes that part of our lives away.

Now there is just an open space
Where that big comfy being used to stand.
(I think of you often, standing in that space.)
And now where your shade was drawn,
I only have the warmth of the almighty
Penetrating sun to remind me
Of what I have lost.

Michelle Norris
Buffalo, NY

The Trees of Fall

Trees are so stately and tall
And give shade to one and all:
They are shelter for the birds that call
And are peaceful just to look upon.

In the Fall they their colors don,
No more beautiful sight to behold,
Than when they are arrayed
In their red, green and gold.

Annette Dorgan, age 90
Bristol Home, Buffalo, NY
(mother of Marjorie Norris,
Grandmother of Marie Norris-Baxter
And Mark Norris)

Rememberings

Joyce Kilmer wrote "Trees", but if you please,
I'll pen a few lines of my own:

My love for the sycamore, maple and birch
Began when I was a kid.

I'd walk down the street, stare up at the leaves,
And see where the red robins lived.

Entering the scene the stately elm
Bowed its lovely head.

By the time I grew up, Dutch Elm sneaked in,
Rendering my old friend dead.

The dogwood still blooms,
The camphor still sweeten,
The oak is mighty as ever.

The sweet gum delights,
Willows bend lowly,
My heart overflows without measure.

Though branches be bare
And pine needles may fall,
I know that my heart is sound.

For in the grand ash, aspen,
Chestnut and larch
My happiness freely abounds

Patricia Horbett
Lancaster, NY and
Land O'Lakes Florida

The Coat Tree

Bent under the weight of winter clothes
The coat tree snapped and
When the coats fell...
Hats rolled.
Hangers careened.
An umbrella stabbed the hardwood floor.
A snowsuit trailing mittens doubled-up
On impact, a rain mac, tartan lining gone
Lunged sideways, as a pair of pants slithered
Down and out of a plastic sleeve—
While on a single hanger, two windbreakers,
Buried since early Fall, under a brown down
Parka, sloughed off in tandem, still yet a castoff
Camel topcoat came down arms spread wide
In its plummet.

J. Tim Raymond
East Aurora, NY

Tree of Life

(For a Tree Overhanging Ellicott Creek at Glen Park)

You had to burst
Through a gray wall
Full-blown
Like Athene through Zeus' gray brain
And lean over
The tumultuous water.
Your pale fans of blossom
Against the white torrent
As white ghost fungi contrast
With the dark limbs they haunt,
You reach out your beds
Like tiny deer hooves
Risking falling into the catastrophic river.
Craning your head up
(like a swimmer to keep breathing)
you struggle against your prone position.
I, too, crane my neck and reach to you,
But I am afraid to go flat out
Over the abyss.

Katharine Tussing
Buffalo, NY

Comrades in Arms

Comrades in arms in weather
Wars waged in Buffalo,
Standing in the line of fire
From lake effect artillery
Unleashed in winter's battles,
Your limbs, once lifted to the sky
In glorious profusion, are broken,
Your wooden shoulders frozen
In downward shrugs of sad defeat.
Like on a war-torn battlefield,
Severed branches and amputations
Have rent and splayed your trunks.
The fusillade from wind and snow
Leaves brown bark shrapnel
Strewn on every lawn.
Your resinous blood of life
Spills on the ground.

Leafy flags in changing colors
Before the solstice darkness,
Are drafted in the irony
Of any early autumn fall.
An infantry of trees stands
At valiant attention,

Decorated veterans, all.
Taken for granted in better times,
These arboreal friends,
Are fallen soldiers, too—
Remembered in pictured archives

And, surely, in our hearts.
Come spring, some may remain,
Sprouting hope with every bud,
Or, be removed forever.

Barbara Nowak
Niagara Falls, NY

City of Trees

Nestled here, between two Great Lakes, Buffalo New York boasts a canopy of green, going back hundreds of years. The famous urban planner, Olmsted, envisioned a network of parks, capitalizing on our bounteous Dutch Elms. A disease overtook the elms in the 30's, but maples, sycamores, and oaks eventually filled in the spaces of Delaware Park and elsewhere.

Former Buffalonians return here from Florida and the Southwest to visit from June through October, just to experience the lush arbors along our streets and parks.

Everywhere I've lived, I always bought a house with the biggest trees on the street, in front or behind my home. I'm a forest person, for that's where my soul soars.

Then came the unprecedented, water-laden snows of October 12th to 13th, 2006! Twenty-two inches of slush in eight hours, lightning lashing, all attacking defenseless, leaf-laden trees.

I lay in my bed that horrible night, when snow-silent air was interrupted by sudden crashes of major limbs breaking off the arbors. I raised my bedroom window shade to investigate, not believing my eyes. The architecture of the sky was tumbling, and that sky was dark, save for the lightning going every which way.

No electricity, no heat, and the house was cooling down. My down comforter kept me reasonably arm, for a while. I felt I would survive the discomfort—but the trees, the birds, the deer, the squirrels, rabbits, untold wildlife—all were suffering a hurricane, losing their homes, in fear of losing their lives.

I've always felt close to trees. When I moved from my old home I hugged every tree on the property, before I went to my car to follow the movers. Now my beloved ornamental pear tree, the one that graces the front of my porch, is a shadow of her former self. Side branches hang out, wanting for a hug, then mourn the center and middle branches, all GONE.

Diana Manus
Amherst, NY

A Cry for the Trees

Standing at the back door
The night of the storm
In between claps of thunder
And heavy falling snow

There is silence
An eerie muteness
Except for the snap of tree limbs
Like gunshots exploding
Or bones breaking

The trees,
Almost peaked in their
Autumn color
Now droop
Buckle
Collapse
From the weight of
Water-laden snow
On those glorious leaves

Limbs submit to the strain
Crash to the ground
One here, there, across the way
All around the neighborhood
The branches continue breaking
Throughout the night

Tomorrow we will survey
The damage of
A landscape maimed
Our scenery severed

Tonight all we can do
Is cry
For the trees

Diane Evans
Grand Island, NY

October trees

They stretch to the ground
Weighted by their whiteness

Their burdened branches
Twist, crack from struggle

Seeking freedom from the storm
They toil and bow from their load

Leaves that should have gone
Stayed fixed

Their pages without words
In nakedness witnessing the storm

Then …flakes melt

Trunks and branches spring back

Randomly rebounding

Then the fixers come

Now the pruner's blade is set upon them

Removing what was

Erasing signs of natures wrath

Clearing the way …..for what ?

Always missing the whole of things

Good and bad complete life's cycle

Sorrow and joy forever partners

Breakage fosters healing
Nature repairs all in its time
Put the Band-Aids away

Timothy Maggio
Buffalo, NY

The Whipping Tree

I see you spying down on me
Your anger, so dark
I see you, your branches
Stiff and hard, your control
So cold.

I see your body swaying
To the wind, your fingers
Like a whip.

I see your dominant self
Appear. You are whipping
Me through the night.

Bobbie Bailey
Buffalo, NY

Trees

Broken
Without limb or leaf
You slump
Like confederate soldiers
On a bloody field of battle

We look at you
With pity and with sadness
Seeing only the devastation,
Seeing only the pain.

Yet...

You hold a secret
Sweet and ancient
Deep deep down
In the mother's
Earthy womb
Moist and safe
Protected from
Fierce winds and driving snow....

Knowing fingers stretch out
Sinewy roots
Strong
And full of life
Search out the
Promise of next spring
And sap rising once again

Pamela Blawat
Buffalo, NY

God's Creation

A tree, bushy and green, trying
To reach out to me through
The window screen.

How I welcome its friendly
Appearance.

God's creation has wonderful
Endurance.

Tall and beautiful, full of life
I hear your message of love
Tonight.

Mary Jo Foley
Williamsville, NY

TREES USED TO SPEAK TO ME MORE THAN THEY DO NOW

That old oak, for instance,
Stolid, yes, dumb as a tree trunk
Most days. Last week
I noticed the tree leaking black stains.
"Is that rot?" I say to it, "Are you going to
Fall on my house in a storm?
Am I going to have to knock you down?"
Not a word from the tree, just
Oozing, and dropping showers of leaves.

The tree had my attention, though.
I thought of the ones I'd climbed,
The maple like a mast I climbed on the high seas
Of my imagination,
The willow whose soft curtains gave me a tearoom.

Now I've hardened and got weighty,
Too stiff to climb,
To heavy to fall.

Wait, a tree house, I think, I need a tree
House and ladder, "Now that's
A better idea" said the tree, finally speaking,
"and enough of the cutting me down talk."

Corky Culver
Melrose, Florida

Prescription: A Fall Road Trip for the End of a Love Affair

Oh deep red, the bright reds, the gold—irony around every
Curve of the Forest Ridge Parkway.

The separation layer between leaf and branch has dissolved.
Leaf is ready to fall or fly depending on the mood of the wind.
Perfect! The tree lets no raw wounds open to infection because
The branch was ready to lose its leaves, in fact, needed to,
(Are we feeling better yet?)

Like a parent sending a baby bird from a nest—
Okay you're ready to fly now—

Or humans who have provided for kids and now need
To be thinking of themselves, maybe need to downsize
And not keep all the kids' old bedrooms ready for when
Their plans don't work out or their marriages
Or their health or their jobs,
And the kids boomerang back home.

I see in the paper
About the ice storm that came early to my friends up North,
Before they were ready, the trees still full of wet full leaves,
Weighted iced limbs cracking, tearing trees apart.
It's easy to come up with a vicarious aching since

I'm like those trees up in Buffalo. I'm not ready, I have a raw wound.
The separation layer in me, that handles these things, wasn't given the time
It needed. It wasn't ready.
I'm not in acceptance. I didn't mean what I said back then.
This I think as this gorgeous Fall ignores me
And I drive along, eating just desserts, in a car full of karma

I stop at an old hotel with merry fires in the lobby and merry couples
On the couches in front of the fires. Trees "ablaze with color" have brought
Us tourists from the South and the city, some ablaze with melancholy
Not immediately visible. "Sing a sad country song," we ask in the piano lounge,
"Those country folk have got it right."

Corky Culver
Melrose, Florida

Touching Cedars

Walking through a grove on the way to a shell mound left by Indians of another century, I began to notice the cedar trees along the way. Cedars always seem to have a look of formal ritual somehow—their dark green in landscapes bleached by winter, in this place, somber against the white sand and white shells. A little reverent or serious or deep or religious or something. They seem to be protectors.

I began to touch each one as I passed. The needles were nubbly, fragrant. It may have been only I myself that changed and awoke, but it seemed that the cedars responded somehow. The path felt different. A lifting, a lightness everywhere.

Folk may call that anthropomorphic or the "pathetic fallacy", ascribing human feelings to nature—some sort of sentimentality. But I'm not sure what the greatest extravagance is, believing trees actually are spirit in some way similar to us or believing they are not.

Corky Culver
Melrose, Florida

Leaves

Fall waters fall, sap pulls back
Rain floods woods and roads
Moisture within the leaf flares before it
Dries. I dream two lovers
Going back and forth and hurting both,
This tree, that tree, in love here, so bright,
In love there, so bright:
It's all over in a few weeks

And we are left bare

No more passions permitted
For any of us. Birds leave the dark
Wet branches bare, no quickening
Of breath, no song, no obsessions
No rivals, no jealousies, no comparisons,
No yearning, no illumination. Gone
The bright colors that unbuttom the
Blouse and kiss the breasts
And heart.

Corky Culver
Melrose, Florida

Two Trees

Two huge maples grace my yard,
Older than my 65-year house, and
Taller than all the rest in Buffalo.

Between them my hammock
Has always swayed in summer,
Like an apron or a pelvis rocking,
Rocking.

On that night in October when
The heavy snows came, and
The winds rocked and thunder
Sounded, I kept running

To my dining room window,
Searching the trees, staring
First at their wide tops,
Then their square trunks.

Amazed, I saw their gracious
Arms leaning toward ground,
Sore, heavy with leaves
And the ache of autumn.

I could not save their boughs
As I heard the Pop! and
Whoosh! of fallen wood
And then the heavy rumble
And crack toward ground.

I could not fully imagine
What was happening
In the dark….

The next day, chest-high
In my yard, their limbs
Touched me for the last time.

It took four hours by myself
To shake each one
By the hand and drag
Them gently to the steet.

Amazingly, these trees
Still stand, tall and proud,
Slimmed down by October's
Storm as if readying themselves

For the El Nino warmth
Of December, and then,
That frozen February. Nature
Knows somehow, or doesn't
Know. You just have
To embrace that instinct.

Marjorie Norris
Buffalo, NY

Sally Johnson's Apple Tree

(reflecting her photograph, page 132)

I am looking at the apple tree
And all the grasses reaching,
The bright sky, almost white
Behind the floating orbs of apples,
The apples dancing, hypnotized
In the morning light, the crate
On the left waiting to be filled.
There are apples bobbing
In the gentle breeze, a child's
Party game, and one or two
Pointing out like suckling breasts.
This, then, is an enchanted tree,
Immeasurably itself, swinging
In the mild air, held staunchly
By its wooded trunk, thick
And solid. If this tree could
Talk, she would say, "Eat me,
Drink me. I'll be all to you,
Great nourishment, profound
Celebration. Finger paint
With my juices, this is life,
Consumable"

Marjorie Norris
Buffalo, NY

Previously published in Resilience
San Diego: Aventine Press 2007

The Trees

It was in soft October light
The color of peaches and of sand
That the storm came, hurling
Down snow like great tufts
Of heavy feathers, weighty snow
That oppressed the fall trees
Full of rosy leaves and thoughts,
Just as autumn would hope
To mature into winter,
Slow and unembarrassed.
And the trees were
Not prepared for cruelty,
As we were not, all
Snow innocents,
Embarking on a new
Planet, full of crunchy
Boughs and soul
Surprises, shifts
In heat and cold,
Shifts in mood
And texture, looking
For some holy clue,
Something we could
Understand, some
Cataclysmic consciousness
Among these felled arbors

Marjorie Norris
Buffalo, NY

The Progenitor

Your skeletal frame
Stands exposed
Dark, bare
Seemingly dead
Evergreen not
Yet you hide
An eternal spring
Backed by the bluest
Skies and the symphony
Of a finch's spring

I gaze and gasp at
Your beauty, the progenitor

Yet standing alone
In the middle meadow
Of spring scattered
In far-off places,
You inspire me
To dream of my eternal spring
That comes after every winter

Jennifer Willett
Kenmore, NY

From My Window

From my window I see
A new Spring growing
From the abruptly cut branch
Of a tall and majestic tree.
        Fall was hell.
I will have to go a few doors
Down to see
What kind of leaves it bore.
        Early Spring:
        It grows well.
Never tell the damage done.
Hope and splendor reigns once more.

Kimberly Beck
North Tonawanda, NY

Dancers and Saints

Trees are like dancers, with long limbs stretching up toward the sky
In a pas de deux with nature, they dance until they die
Swaying with the autumn breeze, they give the wind its sound
While falling leaves, in pirouette, glide gently to the ground

Trees are like dancers, with branches extended in a striking arabesque
In a tango with the elements, putting stamina to the test
They fuse with their environment, roots firmly in the ground
With all their grace and beauty, a poem lovelier could not be found

To all trees that danced in the Surprise Storm of October 13, 2006

Kathy Roth
Buffalo, NY

Blossom Anyway

Does the goldfinch, in mid-whirl,
Suddenly recall an April from years before—
The last happy spring?
Does it regret stolen possibility?

Does the magnolia strive to survive?
Does it measure its thwarted limbs,
Hoard its meager buds unevenly spread
On mishapened stems?

Sadness is yours alone.
Take it as a form of life
Connecting you to soul
As truly as the finch's gold
Flashing across the lilacs.

Cut down, blossom anyway.
Open again along whatever
Branches remain.

Patricia Freres
Buffalo, NY

Listening

The big maple tree in front of my house talked to me.
Not in words but in rebellion with
Showering bud scales,
Twirling propellers,
Clotting leaves,
Tangling roots,
Heaving sidewalks,
Cracking concrete,
Falling bark,
Splitting lawn,
And branches that stretched and clawed at roof shingles.
In early October of 2006 I listened, heard, and called a trimmer,
The first in fifty years,
To prune and cut and shear its unruly mass.
The big maple tree in front of my house still talks to me.
It remains relentless, demanding, insistent.
And I am thankful.

Linda Lavid

Linda A. Lavid is an award-winning author from Buffalo, NY. She has published two collections of short fiction, a novel, and a non-fiction book on writing and publishing. To learn more, please visit lindalavid.com

Healing the Wound

I walk down
An old logging road
Toward the river.
Patches of gravel
Barely show
Through the carpet
Of Queen Anne's lace
And other mountain grasses.
Bits of iron guardrail
Here and there rust
Back into the earth.
Soon the maples and birch
Will sprout saplings
And the forest will
Close back up on itself.
Healing the wound.

Dennis Maloney
White Pine Press
Buffalo, NY

To a Dry Elm

The old elm, split by lightning
And half-rotted
With April rain and May sun,
Has sprouted a few green leaves.

The hundred-year-old elm on a hill
Lapped by the Duero! A yellowish moss
Stains the bleached bark
Of the crumbling, worm-eaten trunk.

Unlike the singing poplars
That guard roads and riverbanks,
It won't be a home to nightingales.

An army of ants in a single line
Climbs up its side and spiders weave
Their gray webs in its hollowed core.

Elm by the Duero, before you are felled
By the woodman's ax and the carpenter
Transforms you into a bell tower,
A wagon axle or cart's yoke;
Before you are a red flame on
Tomorrow's hearth in some poor cottage
Along the side of the road;
Before a whirlwind uproots you,
And the wind from the white sierras snaps you;
Before the river pushes you to the sea
Through the valleys and ravines,
Elm, I want to note
The grace of your green branch.
My heart also waits in hope,
Turned towards light and life,
For another miracle of spring.

Soria 1912 Antonio Machado
Translated by Mary Berg and Dennis Maloney White Pine Press

A Broken Branch

A splintered branch
Without leaf or bark,
Rattling its empty song
In the wind.
Year after year
Tired of living
And dying,
Its song tenacious
Hiding fear.
Another winter,
Another spring.

Dennis Maloney
Buffalo, NY

Not the Same Hereafter

A beautiful autumn afternoon...
A perfect day for a drive back
From Jamestown to Buffalo.

Back goes the sunroof
Allowing in the crisp beauty
Of nature and freedom of life.

Oh look! A fruit stand in the country,
The rust colored squash that calls
Inviting me to bake and enjoy.

Now close to the Thruway entrance,
A sudden and harsh scene change.
Clouds dark and ominous
Roll in quickly and threateningly
Like the wheels of a runaway semi-truck.

Close the sunroof!
Disconnect me from nature-
A dark combination of snow, sleet, hail
Steals my free spirit, joy, and beauty of the day.

Slow down everyone!
The road is quickly a frozen lake
Too dangerous to be near,
Too threatening to drive upon.

Finally I approach the street where I live, or is it?
My knuckles still white, lock tightly around the wheel
As I attempt to maneuver past the gigantic fallen
Tree limbs: they look like a tornado's devastation.

Could it be that just hours ago
Robust autumn leaves adorned

These majestic trees, now weighted by
Heavy snow- covered branches
Slowly disconnecting from their core?

I too am disconnected
From my family
My home, my beautiful autumn drive,
Even my cell phone is not connecting to anyone
And I assume I am home—at last.
The inside looks like the outside—
Dark, cold and ominous.

Once magnificent tree limbs
Lay weeping, grieving on the ground of winter.
They allow no light to enter the house
As the branches are many and thick

They allow no electrical or phone service to flow
How vulnerable we are to nature.
I thank God that all my family is safely home
Although without a generator
How vulnerable we are.

Family, friends, and neighbors
All are welcome---
We'll take care of you...

We quietly talk about the change in landscape
As a result of the storm:
We console each other
As in death of a loved one.

Though we know we are connected,
We will never be quite
The same hereafter

Marilyn J. Ciancio
Producer/Host of National Telly Award-Winning Artscope/Time Warner
2005 Winner: Arts Council of Buffalo and Erie County
2005 Senator Mary Lou Rath Woman of Distinction Award

The Snow is Falling

The snow fell on the grass like circles
Of snow and the grass turned all white.

This is our lilac tree. It got ice on it---
Those things that look like pencils made of
Ice. Me and Eva went out of our house
And felt them. They felt like frozen
Lollipops that you have in summertime.

Auguste Maines, age 4
Buffalo, NY
Bennett Park Montessori School

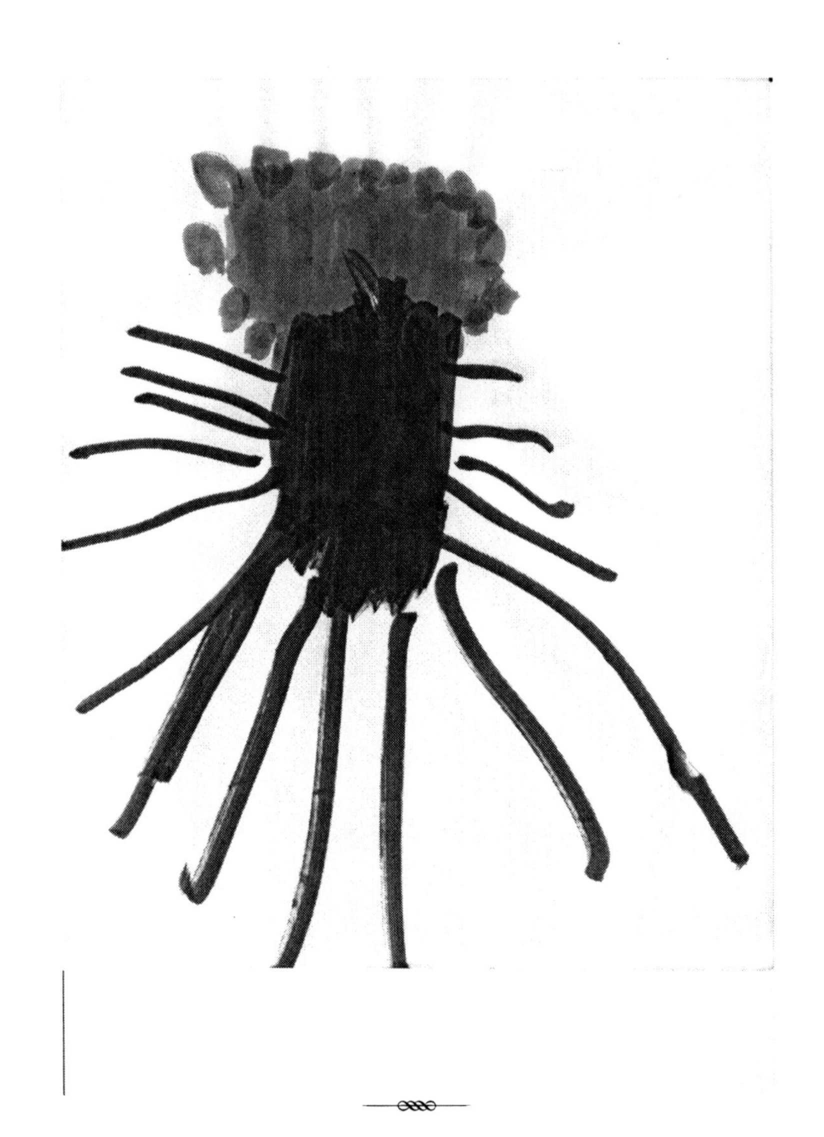

My Blueberry Tree
Eva Maines, age 4
Bennett Park Montessori School
Buffalo, New York

"Tangle"
Priscilla Bowen:

"Unexpected"
Priscilla Bowen:
On exhibit, Collector's Gallery:
Albright-Knox, Buffalo, New York

Talia Roth
Buffalo, New York

Talia Roth
Buffalo, New York

Talia Roth
Buffalo, New York

Talia Roth
Buffalo, New York

Talia Roth
Buffalo, New York

Talia Roth
Buffalo, New York

Talia Roth
Buffalo, New York

Talia Roth
Buffalo, New York

Talia Roth
Buffalo, New York

Talia Roth
Buffalo, New York

Talia Roth
Buffalo, New York

Talia Roth
Buffalo, New York

Talia Roth
Buffalo, New York

Talia Roth
Buffalo, New York

Talia Roth
Buffalo, New York

Talia Roth
Daughter of Kathy Roth
Buffalo, New York

Talia Roth
Buffalo, New York

Talia Roth
Buffalo, New York

Peter Kirsch
Buffalo, New York

James Sedwick, South Wales, New York
Remains

James Sedwick, South Wales, New York
Tree/Shadow

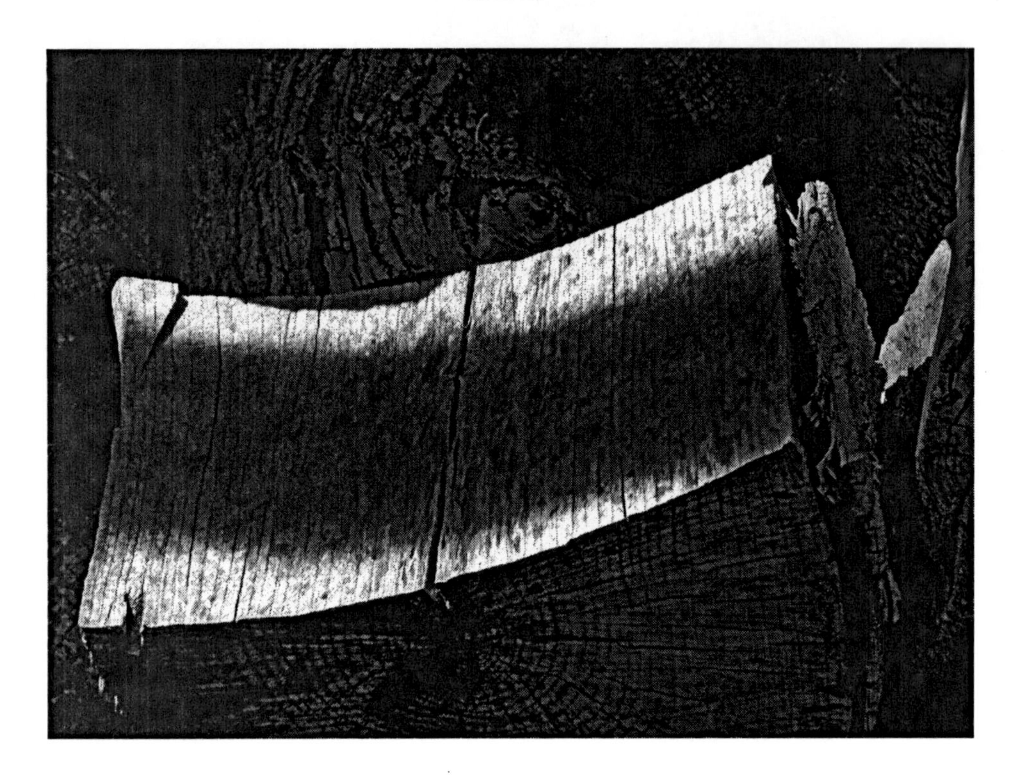

James Sedwick, South Wales, New York
Cut

alive
whisper blossom nest
leaf broken color bird musical
drip
growing protected watched
beautiful waving wind crack snow
struck
brown multi leafed bare heard crying green
laughter shelter bird breeze message green
red taken felt gone bird season beloved
wet frost
shade fed by rain universe yellow palm
remembered a home lifelong seen
remembering
orange protected gentle
a place to go red
watched from under
worried about
wondered
over
tree
sturdy
tree
many-
ringed
tree
leaved-
against
tree
sturdy
tree
widening
tree
embracing
spiraling
home
deep root

Celia White, Buffalo, NY:
Image Poem

Liz Walczak, Alden, New York:
Car, Trees, Road

Liz Walczak, Alden, New York:
The Willows Weep

Liz Walczak Alden, NY:
The Trimming

Liz Walczak, Alden, New York:
Split

Joseph Verrastro:
Cazenovia Park: Early Morning

Joseph Verrastro, South Buffalo, New York: Majestic

Joseph Verrastro, Buffalo, NY:
Trees of Surprise

Katherine Walczak, Alden, New York
Corner of Broadwaynd Schwartz

Judith Witt, Blasdell, New York:
Fall Fantasy

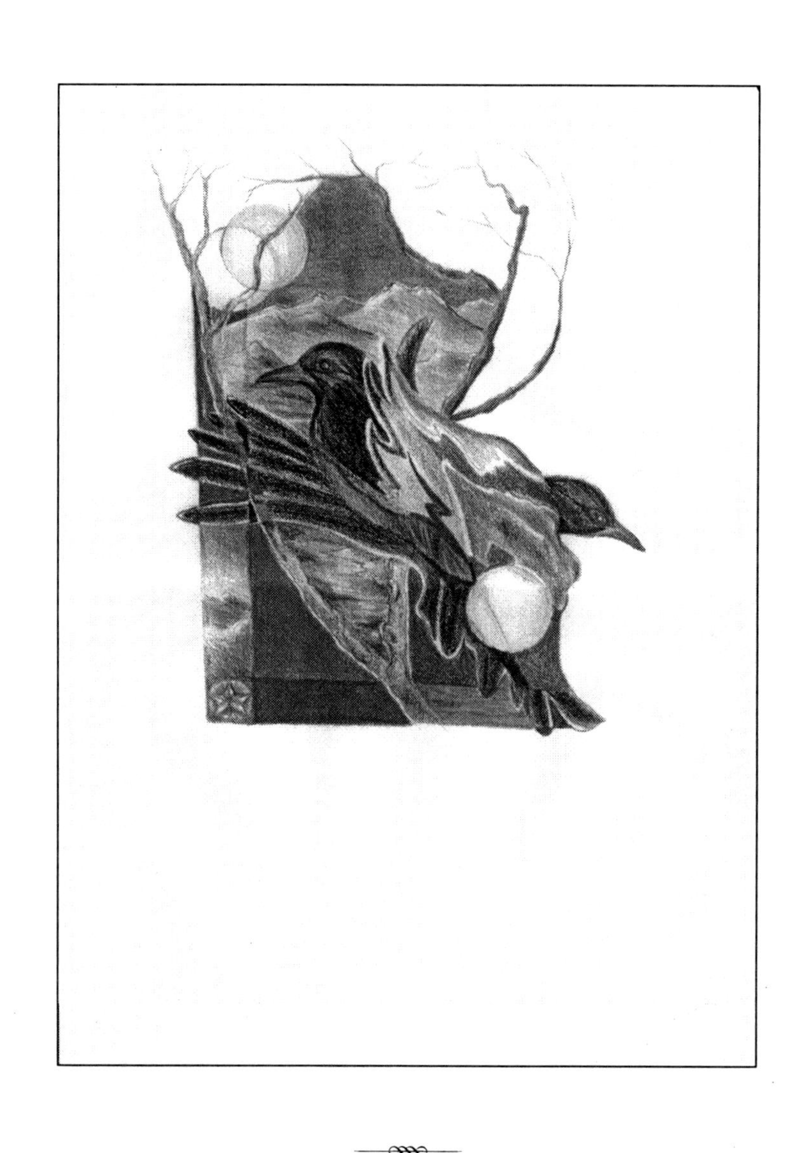

Judith Witt, Blasdell, New York:
Nevermore

Sally Johnson, Gasport, New York
My Favorite Apple Tree

Sally Johnson, Gasport, New York
Winter Apples

Sally Johnson, Gasport, New York
Old Man Winter

Liz Walczak, Alden, New York:
Barn in October's Ice

Author

Photographers

Artists

Made in the USA